GOD HELP ME, I'M GRIEVING

Finding Healing After Loss

KATHERINE B. BARNER

— Foreword by Lee E. Skinner —

GOD HELP ME, I'M GRIEVING

Finding Healing After Loss

KATHERINE B. BARNER
— Foreword by Lee E. Skinner —

RELIANT R
PUBLISHING
A DIVISION OF REDEMPTION PRESS

Published by Redemption Press, PO Box 427, Enumclaw, WA 98022
Toll Free (844) 2REDEEM (273-3336)

Redemption Press is honored to present this title in partnership with the author. The views expressed or implied in this work are those of the author. Redemption Press provides our imprint seal representing design excellence, creative content, and high quality production.

Published 2018
Printed in the United States of America

ISBN-13: 978-1-68314-431-1

Library of Congress Catalog Card Number: 2018930275

DEDICATION

This book is dedicated to the women upon whose
shoulders I stand:
my mother, Norma J. Broussard,
my grandmother, Katherine E. Rines, and
my great-grandmother, Jennie V. Paul.
Because of them, I am.

CONTENTS

ACKNOWLEDGMENTS

Phew! After nearly a year of thinking, praying, writing, stopping, arguing with God, starting again, arguing with God some more, tears, early mornings, and late nights…I did it! This has been one of the most challenging experiences of my life. Trust me when I tell you, writing a book and doing it the right way is not for the faint hearted. There is no way I could have completed this project without the love and support of some amazing people God has placed in my life.

To my husband Celious, thank you for your unwavering love and support. For covering me in prayer when my nerves got the best of me. For being what I never knew I needed.

To my children Breanna and Michael, thank you for cheering me on even when you didn't really know what you were cheering for. Thank you for always giving me a reason to laugh.

To my Uncle Ronnie, thank you for introducing me to Jesus and always challenging me to go deeper in God's word.

To my big brother Reggie, thank you for always having my back and being my biggest fan.

To my Aunt Ann, thank you for being my safe place when I felt the walls of grief closing in on me.

To my sister-cousins Rossie and Vonda, thank you for the late night, early morning, anytime phone calls and text messages reminding me, "You got this baby cousin."

To my Spelman sisters Cindy, Cheryl and Erica, thank you for being my forever friends and the definition of true sisterhood.

To my pastor Lee E. Skinner, thank you for teaching me the truth of God's word and giving me the opportunity to exercise my gift.

To "MDF" Marcia, thank you for always telling me the truth and being my Titus 2 example.

To my friend and publishing consultant Kathy R. Green, thank you for your selfless spirit, your guidance, direction and support throughout this process.

To the entire team at Redemption Press, thank you for taking my dream and making it a reality.

To each and every one of you, I am eternally grateful!

FOREWORD

"I need to make an appointment to sit on the burgundy sofa." This is code for, "God is up to something in my life and we need to talk about it." Katherine Barner whom I affectionately call "K.B." has been a friend and confidante to Marcia and me for the past fifteen years. In that time she has shared with clarity and captivating humor her journey from Orange, TX; time spent at Spelman College in Atlanta, GA earning her bachelor's degree; transitioning to North Texas to complete her master's degree in Counseling; and later forming a family in Houston, TX. Those years have included challenges that stretched the boundaries of her professional training and tested her Christian character. She has provided comfort to others, but as life would have it she has needed comfort of her own…hence, "the burgundy sofa."

Comfort at its core means to make one feel better. Conceptually, it is the desire of most of us to not only give but receive as well. The hope or expectancy in life for better outcomes is often overshadowed by outliers of disappointment. To that end, the ever present shadow of comfort aligns with the need to have our balance restored. The ideal is to bring the practical application of and desire for comfort into a symbiotic relationship. In *God Help Me, I'm Grieving*, Katherine demonstrates how to move the needle from ideal to reality with grace and poise.

The saying, "a picture is worth a thousand words" certainly applies in this case. To personally witness an individual go through the various trials of life that God allows and come out of them with His glory in mind is admirable. A collage of moment to moment snapshots is what Katherine has vividly portrayed in this book.

In a day when many are propounding a gospel of ease and pleasantries, Katherine has given helpful insights to counter that false perception. Her experiences reveal what we can do to manage and survive the symmetry of hope and despair.

In her consistent pursuit of God and His word she is a vital member of our church's teaching ministry. That has been enhanced by her studies at Grace School of Theology. Many individuals of our church family have benefited personally and privately from Katherine's wise, professional counsel.

I believe her words that extend from God's word must be read and applied by anyone who needs to find or wants to give healing after loss. For those grieving right now, prepare yourself to be restored. For those wanting to provide hope, consider this a necessary and valuable resource.

Do it for His glory!
Lee E. Skinner, Pastor
Good Shepherd Baptist Church
Houston, TX

INTRODUCTION

I'm so excited you've decided to embark on this journey. I may not know you, but I've been praying for you. That may sound a bit weird, but as I worked on this project, I prayed for every person who would hold this book in his or her hands. And since you're reading this, that includes you. Now let me share why I started writing at all.

I've counseled countless individuals over the past twenty years whose lives have been shattered by grief in one form or another. With each encounter I discovered a common thread running through the stories of loss. That thread was the search for understanding and healing—understanding of a complex construct with its unsettling twists and turns and healing from its relentless grasp.

I've also had my own run-ins with grief. In the majority of those instances, I was clear on what to do and how to move forward. After all, as the mental health professional, I was supposed to have it all figured out, right? But something changed after my parents died. All the years of experience seemed to fly out the window, and I found myself grasping to make sense of my life. Thankfully, with those years of experience and a strong faith in God, I at least knew where to start. But don't think for a moment my road was easy. Here's what I realized: if I struggled as much as I did to find healing after my own loss and I *knew* all about grief, how in the world was everyone else getting through this unimaginable pain?

That's my why. I got tired of watching people flail in the wind with no clear direction on how to heal. So, I want to provide a resource for you as you seek to understand your loss. I want to give you hope that healing really is possible. I suppose the biggest lesson I want you to gain from this book is that your grief is valid. No one gets to tell you it isn't, and no one gets to tell you how or for how long you should grieve.

I've included parts of my own story throughout the book. I'll be honest; I didn't want to add those for a couple of reasons. The first, because I'm a super private person and I keep things pretty close to the vest. The second, because this isn't about me. It's about you and your journey toward healing. But I realized sharing a bit of myself might just help you see exactly what I'm trying to convey, that what you're experiencing is normal and you are not alone.

In each chapter you'll find practical information, portions of my personal experiences with loss, and plenty of scripture references. I've also included an entire chapter to address dealing with your grief during the holidays. Because let's face it, holidays can be tough to navigate without the people or things that are no longer with us. There is space at the end of each chapter for you to take notes or record your thoughts. Make sure you have a pen and highlighter handy to capture points that jump out at you.

Let me say upfront; grief can be messy and complicated. Finding healing after loss can be hard work. There will be roadblocks and setbacks along the way. There will be times when you'll think the reality of healing is nothing more than a cruel joke. And that's OK. Just keep moving ahead because what I can also say is this, the pain along the way will pale in comparison to the joy you'll experience once you've made it successfully through the process. How do I know? Because I've traveled the road ahead of you and made it safely to the end of my journey. That means you can too!

God bless you as you heal.
Katherine

CHAPTER 1

Unmasking Grief

No matter who you are, where you live, or what you have accomplished, at some point in your life, grief will become a reality for you. It is an inevitable part of living, loving, and acquiring. Grief is often misunderstood, misinterpreted, and its impact minimized. It is, however, a normal human response after any significant loss. It is a process you must move through in order to discover healing and contentment.

Grief comes in many different forms and is expressed in many different ways by each of us. Dealing with grief can be challenging when you do not fully understand its many layers. Having a clear understating of your grief is key to adequately addressing and healing from its effects on your life. There are a few important characteristics vital to obtaining this outcome. I refer to these as the "Three P's of Grief."

Grief Is Perfectly Normal

People often view grief as an abnormal emotional response when in fact it is the exact opposite.

The emotions experienced with grief do not mean you are crazy or weak. The experience of emotion related to your grief does mean you are a normal human being who is in need of healing from your loss.

When grief is treated as an abnormal occurrence, moving forward can pose a significant challenge. Judgmental and unsympathetic responses by well-intended family and friends who do not understand the grief process can hinder your ability to realize true healing. It is important for you to understand, and respect the journey you are on even when others don't. It is not uncommon for those within the Christian community to cause one another to feel that because of your professed faith in Christ you shouldn't grieve. In reality nothing could be farther from the truth. You may hear the following phrases:

- "You should be over that by now."
- "It's been long enough. You need to just move on."
- "Don't cry; you know he or she is in a better place."
- "God wouldn't put more on you than you can bear."

While each of these statements may have some truth to them, it's important as you move along your journey toward healing that you reject the sentiments of others who view your grief as out of the ordinary. I experienced this firsthand several years ago after my father's death. It had been about three weeks since his passing, and I was still experiencing the sadness that came with the finality of that relationship. While talking with my husband one day about how I was feeling, he said, "It's been three weeks. You should be better by now."

Now, let me be completely honest and say my follow-up response was not one that was pleasing to God! And yes, it took more than a few minutes for me to calm down and cool off. But, once that happened, it was crystal clear to me my husband was not trying to send me into orbit. The reality was he simply did not know how to handle my grief in that moment. It made him uncomfortable because he could not fix it.

More often than not, people forwarding these "grieve faster" ideas are in fact having difficulty dealing with your grief and therefore would like for it to end as quickly as possible. The comments you hear regarding moving on, not crying, or placing a time limit on your tears have very little to do with you and far more to do with those around you. After all, grief isn't pretty. It's hard, painful, and can be downright ugly at times.

As difficult as it may be for family and friends to witness your grief, do not apologize for it. It is normal. And it is an important component of your healing. You have the right to grieve in your own way and in your own time.

Grief Is a Process

I don't know anyone who enjoys pain and suffering. On the contrary, when pain arrives on the scene, almost everyone I know wants it gone as quickly as possible. The same is true with grief. Unfortunately, it just doesn't work that way. Healing from grief is a process. This is probably the most difficult aspect of grief to understand.

A common question from people dealing with grief is "how long does it last?" Simply put, it takes as long as it takes, and the timeframe is different for every individual. I know that's not what you want to hear, but it's the truth. There are some common stages you will move through as you heal (we'll cover those in detail later). But those stages are not as simple as one, two, three, and you've arrived at healing. It's a bit more complicated.

Have you ever broken a bone or had surgery? Aside from the initial pain, the healing process can be equally as painful and uncomfortable. My son broke his wrist while skating many years ago. (Side note: I still cringe anytime he tells me he's going skating, and he's an adult now.) At any rate, that broken wrist necessitated a trip to the emergency room, consults with doctors, referrals to an orthopedic specialist, temporary cast, permanent cast, x-rays, pain medication, and months of healing and rehab.

There were times when my son was in no pain at all and struggled to understand why he had to continue wearing the cast. At other times, he was in terrible pain, and the mere thought of moving his arm brought him to tears. No matter how much he wanted to wish it away, he had to go through the process in order for his bone to heal properly. Had we removed the cast prematurely, the likelihood of causing additional damage would have increased. Healing had to take place from the inside out.

What's my point? There will be times when you are in so much pain that it is hard to think about anything else. Other times, the pain will be far less intense, and you'll be able to go about your daily routine seemingly unscathed. Your healing from loss has to take place from the inside out as well.

The grieving process includes everything that occurs in order for you to release the past and move on to new experiences. That does not mean you forget the past. It does mean you are able to move forward with life minus the crippling and at times debilitating pain of your loss. It is common for grief to take at least a year or longer. It takes a full year from the time of your loss to cycle through all the "firsts." The holidays, birthdays, special events, and other important dates that will be experienced for the first time without whomever or whatever is no longer part of your life.

Grief Is Personal

Your movement through the grief process will not look like anyone else's. Each individual has his or her own style of grief. Unfortunately, differences in grieving styles can cause tension in relationships when they are not respected. Arguments can ensue. Harsh words are exchanged. And bitterness is born. While it is true of our culture that we have some institutionalized ways of grieving, we must also bear in mind there is no one right way to grieve. Each individual experiences and expresses his or her loss in a way that is unique due to personality, belief system, support system, and situation.

It's worth noting that there are some differences in the grieving styles of men and women. These differences can help you better understand why an individual may be responding in a particular manner following a loss. However, keep in mind these are gender-specific *tendencies* only and do not mean these are behaviors every man or woman will exhibit during the grief process.

Men typically
- process their grief silently and alone,
- have difficulty allowing themselves to cry,
- need to blame someone or something for their loss,
- have a need to fix the pain of others,
- feel a sense of helplessness.

Women typically
- process grief in conversations with family and friends,
- cry easily,
- focus on understanding why a loss occurred,
- feel a sense of hopelessness,
- want to know how others are feeling.

My husband and I are prime examples of these differences in grieving styles between men and women. Two years after our marriage both his father and my father passed away. Their deaths were a mere two months apart, almost to the day. My father-in-law had been ill for several months, and my husband had spent nearly every week traveling between our home in Texas to his father's home in Alabama helping care for him. On the contrary, my father passed away suddenly with no indication that anything was wrong.

My husband's response to his father's death was typical of many men. He had little desire to share his feelings, cried maybe twice, and was focused on taking care of business. Following the funeral, he wanted to get away from everyone as quickly as possible.

My response to my father's death was very different. The tears seemingly would not stop flowing, and I found great comfort in sharing my pain with trusted friends. Following the funeral, I was overwhelmed with grief but again needed to be around trusted family and friends for support. In both circumstances we were each very much aware of the other's needs and responded to each other based on those needs (minus that one glaring failure I mentioned earlier, for which he quickly redeemed himself). As a result, we were able to move through the grief process in our own way and in our own time.

Just as the grief process is personal for adults, it is as well for children and adolescents. It can be difficult to gauge how children or adolescents are really feeling and if they are processing their feelings of loss appropriately. Adults bear the responsibility of providing a safe and supportive environment for young people to heal from loss. One very important factor to bear in mind is the cognitive, emotional, and spiritual development of each child. Every child is different and should be allowed to express grief in his or her own way and in his or her own time.

Young people may
- have some difficulty verbalizing their feelings of loss,
- develop behaviors that may be deemed inappropriate by adults,

- demonstrate anger toward whomever or whatever they believe is responsible for their loss,
- feel the need to become a caretaker for others,
- have difficulty concentrating on tasks of necessity (i.e., school, homework, etc.).

Remember to be patient and open to adjusting to their individual needs. At every stage of life and development, whether adult or young child, it is vital to remember there is no right way to grieve and there is no wrong way to grieve. There is only *your* way to grieve.

Notes

_____
_____
_____
_____
_____
_____
_____
_____
_____
_____
_____
_____
_____
_____
_____
_____
_____
_____
_____
_____
_____
_____
_____
_____
_____
_____
_____
_____
_____

God Help Me, I'm Grieving

_____
_____
_____
_____
_____
_____
_____
_____
_____
_____
_____
_____
_____
_____
_____
_____
_____
_____
_____
_____
_____
_____
_____
_____
_____

CHAPTER 2

It's about Loss

Repeat this phrase aloud three times:
"Grief is about loss."
"Grief is about loss."
"Grief is about loss."

In most instances when you hear a discussion on grief or of someone grieving, it is related to death. Grief is not exclusive to death, although it can and certainly does set the grief wheel in motion. The tentacles of grief extend much farther than the doorstep of death alone. We'll take a closer look at some of the common losses you may experience. Each one comes with its own set of unique challenges, but all are connected by the common thread of grief needing to be unraveled in order to create a place of healing after loss.

Death

We'll start with death since it, as stated above, is how most people identify grief. Many would argue this is the most devastating form of loss experienced. It signifies the finality of a relationship with no chance of reconnection. Death can occur in any number of ways and with any number of circumstances. This will dictate how you move through the healing process. Some of the factors affecting how you experience grief after the death of a loved one or friend can include

- age of the individual at their death,
- cause of death,
- timing of death,
- relationship status.

My first experience with death was as an eleven-year-old child. I was at choir rehearsal with my mother and grandmother when someone—I don't remember who—came in and announced we needed to get home right away. We arrived to learn my grandfather had suffered a heart attack while sitting on the front porch of the duplex my family shared with him and my grandmother. This was something he did every day and something the two of us did together on a regular basis. I remember being sad but not fully understanding what was happening. My grief was sudden but short lived.

On the contrary, the death of my father was a completely different story. I received a pre-dawn phone call from my uncle telling me I needed to get to the hospital. My uncle is not an alarmist, so I knew from the tone in his voice something was terribly wrong. Within eight hours of that phone call, my father was gone—the result of a ruptured hernia poisoning his entire system—leaving my mother, brother, and I shocked and confused. This time my grief was long, protracted, and complicated. I cycled through each stage of the process on what seemed like a never-ending roller coaster created by the most devious engineer on the planet.

You see, grief will invariably accompany death, but the picture of what it specifically looks like for you will vary greatly depending on the details of your loss. The who, the where, the when, and the how will all play a part in the way you navigate your journey toward healing. Whether you are taken on a sudden but short lived trek down the grief road or on a stomach-turning, mega roller coaster, the ride will eventually end letting you off at a safe place marked healing.

Illness

News of a serious, chronic, or terminal illness can rock you to your core. It is perfectly normal to experience a range of emotions when hit with the news of your own diagnosis or that of a loved one's. Fear and frustration of not having definitive answers to your seemingly unending list of questions can further complicate your situation.

My mother endured seven months of prolonged illness prior to her death. During that time my brother and I watched her decline slowly as a chronic illness caught up with her after years of being kept at bay by excellent doctors, proper medication, sheer refusal to give in, and daily prayer. I recall the sadness in her eyes as she struggled to complete minor tasks for herself all the while struggling to accept her new limitations.

For someone used to doing pretty much what she wanted, when she wanted, and how she wanted, witnessing the gradual loss of her independence was difficult for our entire family. For my brother and I, making the mental and emotional shift from child to parent was daunting yet necessary. We each, in our own way, had to grieve what had been and learn to accept what was our new normal.

As was the case with my mother, the loss of independence, loss of previous level of functioning, and altered plans for the future were all residual effects of her illness. These secondary losses tend to be overlooked by most people and deemed insignificant by others. Notwithstanding, they are important aspects of your grief story. Recognizing them as such and giving yourself the time needed to adjust to a different lifestyle will be an integral part of your healing. Change is never easy and redefining your life can be frightening, but remember what you're experiencing is perfectly normal.

Job Loss

Like it or not, right or wrong, many of us define ourselves by our work. Unemployment—for whatever reason—can lead to a downward spiral in many other areas of your life. Let's face it; if you don't work, your ability to manage the necessities of life can be significantly diminished. This can be particularly difficult for men who are more prone to link their identities with their vocational accomplishments. But they do not by any means have the market cornered in this area.

I was fired from a job a few years back, and it absolutely devastated me. The circumstances were undeniably unjust, and it was the first time in my over twenty-year professional career I had been the target of a smear campaign and had my integrity questioned.

Following that incident I found myself cycling through the grief process once again. It paled in comparison to the death of my parents, but it was still immensely painful and required a time of healing. I didn't talk to many people. I was reluctant to trust anyone. I questioned how my career would be affected. I began second guessing nearly everything I had done. Finally, I allowed myself permission to grieve and began moving through the process at my own pace. It wasn't an extended journey but was a journey nonetheless. Interestingly enough, once I arrived at a place of healing, I was able to identify the blessing that was hidden in my loss.

When you face the end of an employment season, whether voluntary or involuntary, you may very well grieve for a time over what has been lost. You may go through a myriad of emotions causing more distress than expected. Whether it's the realization of the professional relationships that will come to an end, your financial stability being threatened, or the loss of a certain status you enjoyed as a result of your occupation, the loss of employment can be an extremely unsettling time in your life. Don't fall into the trap of thinking your feelings are not valid. Doing so can serve to further complicate an already difficult and trying season in your life. Allow yourself permission to experience whatever feelings may arise. Refuse to minimize your emotions for fear that your experience may not fit someone else's model of what qualifies as a grief-worthy event. Your circumstance matters, and your ability to move forward and operate from a place of strength rather than defeat depends on the time and attention given to your healing.

Natural Disasters

I've lived along the Texas Gulf Coast my entire life. Over the past several years, we've had our share of disastrous hurricanes to contend with. My immediate family has been spared much of the destruction brought on by these storms. However, countless other relatives and friends have had to deal with their calamitous effects. Homes, cars, furniture, heirlooms, pictures, clothing, memories—the list goes on and on— have been swept away by torrential rain, wind, and floods.

Hurricanes, of course, are not alone in their ability to annihilate a lifetime of possessions and memories. There are wildfires that rage with unimaginable intensity and tornadoes that swirl sucking up everything in their paths as well as blizzards, mudslides, and tsunamis. Regardless of the form these acts of nature take, their catastrophic effects are without question life altering.

I've counseled numerous families and individuals through the years who entered my office confused about the intensity of emotions felt as a result of loss caused by a natural disaster. Many felt guilty about having such an intense reaction to the loss of material items. However, the reaction was rarely about the item but rather what the item represented.

The greatest obstacle to overcome in these situations is acknowledging these events are completely outside of your control. They often come with little to no warning. In instances where there may be some time to prepare for their arrival, the trail of destruction left behind can linger long after the wind, rain, fire, or waters have ceased. If you've had your life turned upside down as a result of nature's powerful hand, your loss is real, and your grief is valid. Treat it as such so your healing can be complete.

Relationships

I don't think I need to tell you that breakups are hard. The loss of a significant relationship whether romantic or plutonic can be extremely stressful and cause you to grieve the loss of the previous life you once knew. Even if the relationship was not particularly healthy, you may still have an intense emotional response when it comes to an end.

The end of my first marriage was devastating. I recall the flood of emotion swarming my body as the sound of an unknown judge's voice synchronized with the crash of his gavel, declaring my marriage officially over. As I exited "stage left," the highlight reel of what was and what could have been played on a loop in my head while my ears rang from the life-changing symphony I had just heard.

With the loss of any relationship comes the realization of other peripheral losses as well. Events that were once simple and joyous can become overwhelming and complicated.

You may be faced with learning new ways of engaging with family and friends who may or may not understand, agree with, or support the breakup of your relationship.

The new reality of having to schedule time with your children when you once had unfettered access can be undeniably difficult to accept. A loss in financial stability or of the lifestyle you have grown accustomed to are very real and poignant reminders of your loss. Letting go of plans you had for the future, even if only temporarily, can lead to feelings of anger and sadness.

Don't be caught off guard by a period of grief following the loss of a meaningful relationship. It is an indication that you were in some way deeply connected to another human being. Allow the grief process to run its course so that you are better prepared for the next relationship. Embrace it as you look for signs of healing along the way. There will always be clarity and perspective at the end of your journey. It will be a welcome replacement to the pain you once knew.

Notes

_____
_____
_____
_____
_____
_____
_____
_____
_____
_____
_____
_____
_____
_____
_____
_____
_____
_____
_____
_____
_____
_____
_____
_____
_____
_____

God Help Me, I'm Grieving

_____

_____

_____

_____

_____

_____

_____

_____

_____

_____

_____

_____

_____

_____

_____

_____

_____

_____

_____

_____

_____

_____

_____

_____

_____

CHAPTER 3

Riding the Waves of Grief

In 1969 Swiss-American psychiatrist Elizabeth Kubler-Ross introduced the five stages of dying. Her work was precipitated by what she deemed a lack of understanding among medical professionals as it related to individuals in the later stages of life. Kubler-Ross felt there was a lack of emphasis placed on the emotional response of the dying individual. As such, she developed the five-stage model to help better understand the process individuals move through prior to death.

Recognizing the need to expand on her original work, Kubler-Ross later adapted the stages of dying to include stages of grief. In so doing, she provided the framework used today to better understand how individuals move through the grief process. We are able to use this model not only for grief brought on by death but also as the result of any type of loss.

One of the struggles with the idea of grief occurring in stages is the presumption that those stages occur in a step by step, one, two, three linear progression. This is a false assumption that can complicate the healing process by leading people to believe they are grieving incorrectly. Grief does not happen in a neat, orderly emotional vacuum. It takes place in a much more chaotic and unorganized fashion.

Through the years working with clients dealing with loss, I have come to prefer a slightly different way of describing the emotional journey of grief. It's one that resembles a surfer battling unrelenting waves in the vast ocean, while attempting to make it safely to shore. Some of those waves can be navigated with no problem at all. They roll in without much power and allow the surfer to float along until the next one arrives. Others come rushing over head with minimal warning threatening to swallow him or her alive. The size and magnitude of the waves power make it impossible to imagine a safe arrival will ever be reality. This is how the emotions associated with your grief journey will show up. Let's take a look at some of the most common waves you will encounter.

Denial

Denial is the first wave that may roll in. This is where, as the name implies, you may have trouble acknowledging the loss really occurred. You may feel that nothing makes sense and feel overwhelmed by the magnitude of your loss. You may question how or if you will be able to move on.

You may have trouble figuring out why you should move on. You're not living day to day but rather minute to minute. The grief you experience will come at you in waves, and in a strange way denial helps you survive the initial shock of your loss. Processing all the pain at one time can be overwhelming and too much for you to handle. Isn't it interesting how God has created you to handle only a little emotional pain at a time? This is a gracious design indeed.

I counseled an elderly lady a few years ago whose husband had been tragically killed in an on-the-job accident. She shared with me her reaction when her husband's supervisor and company representative arrived at her home to deliver the life-changing news. She responded to the sound of a faint knock at her door followed by a ring of the doorbell that she described as "the sound when someone really doesn't want to make a lot of noise so they half push your doorbell." Answering the door, she observed the two men standing on her doorstep, eyes red from crying and adjusting their footing to appear in full control. She says she closed the door, retreated to her bedroom, and refused to come out until they were gone. She refused to believe the account of events they had come to share with her. This type of response is not uncommon during the denial phase.

While denial serves a purpose in the early stage of grief, the feelings and emotions that are just underneath the surface do eventually find their way to the tip of the proverbial iceberg. When they do, they cannot be ignored. They must be dealt with in order for true healing to take place in your life. Don't be surprised by them. Be prepared for them.

Anger

Anger is another wave that may roll in during your grief process. While riding this wave you may find yourself asking the question: "Why did this happen to me?" You may try to find someone or something to blame for your loss. You may begin feeling like the loss was totally unfair. You may unknowingly displace your anger onto others during this stage of the grief process.

I recall being overtaken by this wave many years ago after my maternal grandmother passed away. Her sister had put her life on hold in California to move to Texas and care for my granny. A few days after the funeral my aunt stopped by our house for a visit. To my dismay she was wearing my grandmother's favorite yellow sun dress! How dare she wear my granny's dress? I was livid, and for months I didn't talk to my aunt. *Over a dress*. But it really had nothing to do with the dress and everything to do with my grief. Furthermore, it never occurred to me that wearing my granny's dress was part of my aunt's grief journey as well.

It's worth noting that God may very well be the target of some or all of your anger. When Lazarus, the brother of Mary and Martha died, Jesus was met by both sisters with the same response: "Lord, if You had been here, my brother would not have died" (John 11:21, 32). Jesus' response to these grieving sisters was one of compassion and love. If you find yourself angry with God, it's OK. He can handle it.

If you find yourself struggling to gain your footing while battling the wave of anger after a loss, recognize it's really hurt turned inside out. It's usually much easier to demonstrate anger than to allow yourself to be vulnerable and communicate the depth of your pain. I tell those I counsel that the issue is never that you become angry but rather what you do with that anger. God never told us not to be angry. He told us not to sin *when* we get angry: "Be angry and do not sin" (Eph. 4:26).

Acknowledge what you're feeling and share your emotions with a trusted friend or family member. As you do, it will help you continue to move through the grief process and closer toward healing.

Bargaining

This wave could easily be renamed the "Please, God" wave. It is where you are unashamed to verbalize your desire to do anything to change your current circumstance and have your life return to your previous state of normal. You may find yourself wishing you or your loved one had gone to the doctor sooner, received the diagnosis sooner, been willing to work on your marriage, made a better financial decision, etc. David found himself in this stage prior to the death of his infant son: "'The child that is born to you shall surely die.' . . . And the Lord struck the child that Uriah's wife bore to David, and it became ill. David therefore pleaded with God for the child, and David fasted and went in and lay all night on the ground" (2 Sam. 12:14-16).

This wave can include a secondary what-if wave in your grief process. It's here that many of your thoughts are consumed with making sense of your loss and its associated pain. Questions focused on what could have been done differently to alter the outcome of your situation are prevalent. Those questions are OK. Ask them, but don't allow yourself to become consumed by them when there is no answer. In most cases, there really is no answer, and that can be beyond frustrating. Allow yourself the room and the grace to ask the unanswerable question and feel the frustration it leaves behind. All of this is important for your healing.

Depression

This may be the most difficult of all the waves. You may experience sudden and intense feelings of loss, hopelessness, frustration, and sadness. There may be times when you feel as if these feelings will never end. Although it may feel as though this wave will last forever, I promise you, it won't. Your feelings are an appropriate response to the pain of your loss.

One of the things I share with individuals during counseling about this particular wave is the fact that they are hurting deeply is not on its face cause for significant concern. It is yet another indication of moving through the grief process. Too often, individuals are made to feel this wave is abnormal. It is not. It is a normal part of the grief and healing process. *Not* experiencing some intense emotions after a significant loss is actually what would fall in the abnormal category.

Listen to the words of Job after experiencing the loss of everything he had acquired, including his ten children, all of his animals, and many of his servants.

"May the day perish on which I was born,
And the night *in which* it was said,
'A male child is conceived.'
May that day be darkness;
May God above not seek it,
Nor the light shine upon it.
May darkness and the shadow of death claim it;
May a cloud settle on it;
May the blackness of the day terrify it.
As for that night, may darkness seize it;
May it not rejoice among the days of the year,
May it not come into the number of the months.
Oh, may that night be barren!
May no joyful shout come into it!
May those curse it who curse the day,
Those who are ready to arouse Leviathan.
May the stars of its morning be dark;
May it look for light, but *have* none,
And not see the dawning of the day;
Because it did not shut up the doors of my *mother's* womb,
Nor hide sorrow from my eyes."
(Job 3:3-10)

These are undeniably words of despair and depression verbalized by a man who according to God himself was a "blameless and upright man." (Job 1:1, 8)

There is a distinction to be made between depression associated with grief and clinical depression. Generally speaking, the intense feelings of sadness and other symptoms associated with grief will decrease over time and come in waves. There will be times when you will feel just fine and other times when you will experience profound sadness. Difficulty sleeping, decreased energy, feelings of frustration, changes in appetite, and trouble concentrating are all symptoms you may experience.

Clinical depression may present with very similar symptoms. However, they tend not to improve with time and when untreated will worsen overtime. Unlike depression associated with grief, clinical depression is persistent, pervasive, and much more severe. It is not dependent on where you are or who you're with. As you move through the grief process, if you are concerned about depressive symptoms that do not appear to be improving, talk to your doctor or a licensed counselor about your symptoms.

Acceptance

There is often misunderstanding about this wave. Acceptance does not mean you are now happy about your loss. It means you have come to a place in your healing where you are able to deal with your loss void of the crippling pain. While maneuvering on this wave you will begin to develop your new normal and look for ways to create new memories. It is where you begin to recognize healing is actually possible. You are less resistant to change and will become open to new ideas, new opportunities, and new relationships that bring you joy. Your thoughts will be filled with more pleasant memories of your loss rather than remaining laser focused on the event which caused your loss.

David demonstrated what acceptance looks like following the death of his young son.

> So David arose from the ground, washed and anointed himself, and changed his clothes; and he went into the house of the Lord and worshiped. Then he went to his own house; and when he requested, they set food before him, and he ate. Then his servants said to him, "What *is* this that you have done? You fasted and wept for the child *while he was* alive, but when the child died, you arose and ate food."

> And he said, "While the child was alive, I fasted and wept; for I said, 'Who can tell *whether* the Lord will be gracious to me, that the child may live?' But now he is dead; why should I fast? Can I bring him back again? I shall go to him, but he shall not return to me." (2 Sam. 12:20-23)

In the case of death you will be able to remember farther back than the circumstances surrounding your loved one's death and remember instead times of laughter, happiness, and joy. There may still be tears, but they will be different tears—tears mixed with smiles of pleasant memories. Enjoy those times. Embrace those times. Look forward to those times. Simply put, acceptance is learning to live again. You can and you will. Trust the process.

As you encounter the various emotional waves your grief will inevitably give rise to, keep in mind you aren't on this journey alone. Remember the story of Jesus and his disciples crossing the Sea of Galilee and being met by a terrible storm? Remember the disciples being so frightened they woke Jesus from what was probably a really good nap? The problem the disciples had was allowing their emotions to override the facts of their situation. They completely forgot what Jesus told them before the journey began.

> On the same day, when evening had come, He said to them, "Let us cross over to the other side." (Mark 4:35)

Jesus had already declared they were going to the other side of the sea. Not only were the disciples going, but Jesus was going too. Therefore, it was impossible for the waves to overtake the boat. Allow that to comfort you regardless of how tumultuous the emotional waves of grief become. God has not left you to journey through your grief alone. He is right there, riding the waves with you and he will not allow them to overtake you.

Notes

_____
_____
_____
_____
_____
_____
_____
_____
_____
_____
_____
_____
_____
_____
_____
_____
_____
_____
_____
_____
_____
_____
_____
_____
_____
_____
_____

_____

_____

_____

_____

_____

_____

_____

_____

_____

_____

_____

_____

_____

_____

_____

_____

_____

_____

_____

_____

_____

_____

_____

_____

CHAPTER 4

The Faith Factor

There is a growing conundrum within the Christian community as it relates to grief and faith. Many have erroneously been made to believe that the expression of real emotions associated with loss somehow nullifies professed faith in an all-powerful God. The challenge then is accepting that the two do not have to be mutually exclusive. There is a both-and component to faith and grief.

Compounding the problem, at times, are the unrealistic expectations of fellow brothers and sisters in Christ. Perhaps you have experienced this struggle. It comes with an unspoken tone from someone that says, "If your faith was stronger, you wouldn't still be grieving" or "Maybe you should pray more." There are some who would have you believe your expression of grief as a Christian is wrong. If those who ascribe to this belief are correct (and they're not), that would mean Jesus was wrong for the way he handled the news of those close to him dying.

After hearing about the murder of his relative John the Baptist, Jesus went away for a time by himself.

> And the king was sorry; nevertheless, because of the oaths and because of those who sat with him, he commanded *it* to be given to *her.* So he sent and had John beheaded in prison. And his head was brought on a platter and given to the girl, and she brought *it* to her mother. Then his disciples came and took away the body and buried it, and went and told Jesus.
> When Jesus heard *it*, He departed from there by boat to a deserted place by Himself.
> (Matt. 14:9-13)

When he heard of the death of his friend Lazarus, Jesus expressed sadness.

> Then, when Mary came where Jesus was, and saw Him, she fell down at His feet, saying to Him, "Lord, if You had been here, my brother would not have died."
> Therefore, when Jesus saw her weeping, and the Jews who came with her weeping, He groaned in the spirit and was troubled. And He said, "Where have you laid him?"
> They said to Him, "Lord, come and see."
> Jesus wept. (John 11:32-35)

Jesus's compassion and tears were a representation of his humanity. He shared an unique and personal relationship with John the Baptist. He was also close friends with not only Lazarus but his sisters as well. And although he knew he would raise Lazarus from the dead eight verses later, the grief endured by his friends was not lost on him during their time of distress.

Scripture is filled with examples of God's children experiencing the same emotions you may be facing today. I want to take you on a walk through scripture to provide you with some solid evidence. We'll call this your faith defense. It will be your ironclad argument against anyone (including yourself) who attempts to make you believe your faith nullifies your right to express your loss.

Job

The book of Job is the most comprehensive example of individual suffering in scripture. Job is referred to as "a blameless and upright man, one who fears God and shuns evil." (Job 1:1, 8) God refers to him as "My servant Job" throughout the book. (Job 1:8, 2:3, 42:7-8) Yet he allows calamity of every kind to find its way to Job's address. In the course of two chapters, this servant of God is transformed from a man at the top of his game, filled in every area of his life, to one stripped of everything he had acquired and barely clinging to life. You should pay close attention to his response to this unimaginable circumstance. Although Job was solid in his faith in God, he still expressed real, poignant pain while seeking to understand the magnitude of his loss. We heard from him in an earlier chapter during our discussion on the waves of grief. It's worth taking a closer look into this book to help you as you work to reconcile your faith and your expression of grief.

"*Why* did I *not* die at birth?
Why did I not perish when I came from the womb?
Why did the knees receive me?
Or why the breasts, that I should nurse?
For now I would have lain still and been quiet,
I would have been asleep;
Then I would have been at rest."
(Job 3:11-13)

"My soul loathes my life;
I will give free course to my complaint,
I will speak in the bitterness of my soul."
(Job 10:1)

"Why then have You brought me out of the womb?
Oh, that I had perished and no eye had seen me!
I would have been as though I had not been.
I would have been carried from the womb to the grave.
Are not my days few?
Cease! Leave me alone, that I may take a little comfort,
Before I go *to the place from which* I shall not return,
To the land of darkness and the shadow of death,
A land as dark as darkness *itself*,

As the shadow of death, without any order,
Where even the light *is* like darkness."
(Job 10:18-22)

The depth of Job's pain resulting from his loss caused him to question why he was ever born and long for death. Throughout the book he sways back and forth between anguish-filled soliloquys aimed at his friends and his God. Yet there are glimpses of Job's continued faith in God even in the midst of his darkest hours.

And he fell to the ground and worshiped. And he said:
"Naked I came from my mother's womb,
And naked shall I return there.
The Lord gave, and the Lord has taken away;
Blessed be the name of the Lord."
(Job 1:20b-21)

"For I know *that* my Redeemer lives,
And He shall stand at last on the earth;
And after my skin is destroyed, this *I know*,
That in my flesh I shall see God,
Whom I shall see for myself,
And my eyes shall behold, and not another.
How my heart yearns within me!"
(Job 19:25-27)

David

Arguably one of the greatest among those who led the nation of Israel, King David experienced significant loss throughout his life and reign. His outward expression of grief upon learning of the death of those closest to him—Saul, Jonathan, and his own son Absalom—is riveting. Although David and Saul shared an undeniably tumultuous relationship, he was no less pained at the knowledge of Saul's life coming to a tragic end just as it did for Jonathon and Absalom.

> Therefore David took hold of his own clothes and tore them, and so *did* all the men who *were* with him. And they mourned and wept and fasted until evening for Saul and for Jonathan his son, for the people of the Lord and for the house of Israel, because they had fallen by the sword. (2 Sam. 1:11-12)

> Then David lamented with this lamentation over Saul and over Jonathan his son . . . (2 Sam. 1:17)

> Then the king was deeply moved, and went up to the chamber over the gate, and wept. And as he went, he said thus: "O my son Absalom—my son, my son Absalom—if only I had died in your place! O Absalom my son, my son!"
> And Joab was told, "Behold, the king is weeping and mourning for Absalom." (2 Sam. 18:33-19:1)

The Patriarchs

Upon inspection of the lives of the patriarchs within the pages of Genesis, it is clear they were not exempt from the pain of grief. Each one demonstrated the significance of his heartbreak with overpowering passion. Death entered their respective circles of influence, leaving a permanent scar where life once resided.

Abraham

"So Sarah died in Kirjath Arba (that *is*, Hebron) in the land of Canaan, and Abraham came to mourn for Sarah and to weep for her" (Gen. 23:2).

Jacob

After being presented with Joseph's bloody tunic and led to believe he had been killed, "Jacob tore his clothes, put sackcloth on his waist, and mourned for his son many days. And all his sons and all his daughters arose to comfort him; but he refused to be comforted, and he said, 'For I shall go down into the grave to my son in mourning.' Thus his father wept for him" (Gen. 37:34-35).

Joseph

At the death of his father, Jacob, "Joseph fell on his father's face, and wept over him, and kissed him" (Gen. 50:1).

More Old Testament Examples

Naomi

Upon returning to Bethlehem after the death of her husband and two sons, "she said to them, 'Do not call me Naomi; call me Mara, for the Almighty has dealt very bitterly with me. I went out full, and the Lord has brought me home again empty. Why do you call me Naomi, since the Lord has testified against me, and the Almighty has afflicted me?'" (Ruth 1:20-21).

Ephraim

"The sons of Ephraim *were* Shuthelah, Bered his son, Tahath his son, Eladah his son, Tahath his son, Zabad his son, Shuthelah his son, and Ezer and Elead. The men of Gath who were born in that land killed them because they came down to take away their cattle. Then Ephraim their father mourned many days, and his brethren came to comfort him" (1 Chron. 7:20-22).

Joash

When he heard of Elisha's terminal illness, "Joash the king of Israel came down to him, and wept over his face, and said, 'O my father, my father, the chariots of Israel and their horsemen!'" (2 Kings 13:14).

Hezekiah

> In those days Hezekiah was sick and near death. And Isaiah the prophet, the son of Amoz, went to him and said to him, "Thus says the Lord: 'Set your house in order, for you shall die, and not live.'"

> Then he turned his face toward the wall, and prayed to the Lord, saying, "Remember now, O Lord, I pray, how I have walked before You in truth and with a loyal heart, and have done *what was* good in Your sight." And Hezekiah wept bitterly. (2 Kings 20:1-3)

God never disqualified anyone for expressing his or her grief. And you are no different. Your emotional response to your loss does not disqualify you as his child. Stand confidently on God's word knowing that he has not forgotten you in your pain and will be with you every step of the way.

> The Lord *is* near to those who have a broken heart,
> And saves such as have a contrite spirit.
> (Ps. 34:18)

> You have turned for me my mourning into dancing;
> You have put off my sackcloth and clothed me with gladness.
> (Ps. 30:11)

Be assured that expressing the pain associated with grief is not an indicator of your level of faith or lack thereof. It is an indicator of your humanity, of your choice to love and be loved. Continue walking in faith toward your healing.

Notes

_____
_____
_____
_____
_____
_____
_____
_____
_____
_____
_____
_____
_____
_____
_____
_____
_____
_____
_____
_____
_____
_____
_____
_____
_____

God Help Me, I'm Grieving

_____

_____

_____

_____

_____

_____

_____

_____

_____

_____

_____

_____

_____

_____

_____

_____

_____

_____

_____

_____

_____

_____

_____

_____

_____

CHAPTER 5

Healing Is Possible

The brutal truth is grief hurts, and you may be wondering how you will ever heal. The natural question you may be asking is "how in the world do I get through this?" The simple answer is "one day at a time." As I've stated earlier, this is not a process that is without bumps in the road and stops along the way. Healing comes in different forms for every individual. But there are some common activities to guide you along the path.

As you learned in the previous chapter, your spiritual health is one area that may take a huge blow during times of loss. A way to minimize the effects of that blow and maintain your spiritual stability is to focus on the following acronym:

G – Go to God in prayer daily.

R – Read God's word daily.

I – Imitate Christ's character.

E – Expect God's deliverance.

F – Fellowship with other believers.

This formula is rooted in the belief that your spiritual health is indeed an integral part of your healing. You can use this formula at any point in the grief process and in any order you choose. You may choose to focus on only one area, or you may want or need to embrace more than one at a time. Regardless of how you follow the formula, it's important to remember your healing is extremely personal and must be treated with care. Let's take a closer look at how G-R-I-E-F can aide you in creating a new perspective.

Go to God in Prayer Daily

You are God's child and therefore have direct access to him. Jesus teaches that as long as you abide in him you can ask whatever you want and it will be done: "If you abide in Me, and My words abide in you, you will ask what you desire, and it shall be done for you" (John 15:7).

This is a definitive statement based on your condition of abiding in Christ. When my children were small and they had a problem or were in pain, they always came to me for help. When I asked, "What do you want me to do?" Their response was invariably "I want you to fix it!" They came to me as their parent because they believed I had the ability to fix whatever was going wrong with or for them.

The same is true for you as a child of God. He should be your first point of contact when you are in pain rather than a last resort. How many times have you phoned a friend before going to God? Your friends and family certainly serve a purpose on your journey of healing, but they should not be the first stop. That place is reserved for God because he is the only one who has the power to heal the pain of your loss. Tell God you are hurting, and ask him to help you heal. When you do, you'll find Paul's words in Phil. 4:6-7 to be true.

> "Be anxious for nothing, but in everything by prayer and supplication, with thanksgiving, let your requests be made known to God; and the peace of God, which surpasses all understanding, will guard your hearts and minds through Christ Jesus."

Read God's Word Daily

You may very well be feeling like this is all too much. You may not feel like praying and definitely not reading anything in the midst of your grief. Here's why you have to fight like crazy not to neglect this part of your healing process. When you're hurting, you are a prime target for the enemy's attacks and lies. You are in an extremely vulnerable state. As such, you have to store up something to help combat the arrows that will be thrown at you in an attempt to keep you in a state of perpetual grief. Remember after Jesus's baptism Satan came to him three times and misconstrued God's word. Jesus's rebuttal was with truth. You must do the same. You have to become what I call an "it is written" warrior. When those negative thoughts begin creeping in about why you lost your job, why you became ill, why your loved one died, or why your relationship failed, you must have a rebuttal based on the truth of scripture.

I will meditate on Your precepts,
And contemplate Your ways.
I will delight myself in Your statutes;
I will not forget Your word.
(Ps. 119:15-16)

For He Himself has said, "I will never leave you
nor forsake you." So we may boldly say:
"The Lord *is* my helper;
I will not fear.
What can man do to me?"
(Heb. 13:5b-6)

The Lord will strengthen him on his bed of illness;
You will sustain him on his sickbed.
(Ps. 41:3)

For I know the thoughts that I think toward you,
says the Lord, thoughts of peace and not of evil,
to give you a future and a hope.
(Jer. 29:11)

Imitate Christ's Character

When you are grieving, the unfortunate truth is you may not be as loving as you otherwise would be. It is certainly understandable that your level of tolerance may be shorter due to the stress of your loss. You may not be desirous of engaging in what you deem to be trivial conversations or activities. Things that would ordinarily not bother you at all may legitimately get on your nerves. You may even feel your negative behavior while grieving is justified. All of this is normal and to be expected to some degree. However, your pain does not provide a free pass to respond or behave in ways that are contrary to God's word. In spite of your loss, there must still be an expectation of holiness and a demonstration of Christ's character.

> But as He who called you *is* holy, you also be holy in all *your* conduct, because it is written, "Be holy, for I am holy." (1 Pet. 1:15-16)

> He who says he abides in Him ought himself also to walk just as He walked. (1 John 2:6)

One of the most common ways to dishonor God during your grief is through your speech. The old adage "sticks and stones may break my bones but words can never hurt me" is simply not true. The sting of harsh words spoken from a place of pain and frustration can linger long after they have left your tongue. Be vigilant and guard against falling into this trap of speaking to others out of your pain and causing unnecessary and at times irreversible damage to your relationships. When you find yourself struggling in this area, it's important to reflect on God's instructions to you.

> A wholesome tongue *is* a tree of life,
> But perverseness in it breaks the spirit.
> (Prov. 15:4)

Let your speech always *be* with grace, seasoned with salt, that you may know how you ought to answer each one. (Col. 4:6)

If anyone among you thinks he is religious, and does not bridle his tongue but deceives his own heart, this one's religion *is* useless. (James 1:26)

Expect God's Deliverance

As you have learned in previous chapters, grief can significantly dim your outlook on life. The overwhelming feelings accompanied with grief can cause your vision to be skewed and can even blind you at times to the possibility of a better and brighter future. When this occurs, you must remain in a place of expectancy based on what you know about God and what he has said in his word. Expectancy says, "OK, God, I don't know how you're going to heal my hurt, but I know that you will." That is a very different statement than "God, I need you to heal my hurt in this very specific way." The danger in the latter statement is God rarely moves in the exact way you want him to but that doesn't mean he won't move at all. Remember, God knows what's best for you and how to best heal you. You have to trust that he really does know best.

"For My thoughts *are* not your thoughts,
Nor *are* your ways My ways," says the Lord.
"For *as* the heavens are higher than the earth,
So are My ways higher than your ways,

And My thoughts than your thoughts.
(Isa. 55:8-9)

Because God knows best, you can expect him to deliver you from the pain of loss.

Fellowship with Other Believers

Grieving in isolation is a bad idea. No matter how much you may want to be left alone, it is not what's best for you. God created you in community and for community. As you move through the grief process, part of your healing will come from fellowship with others. Scripture provides clear instruction to believers on comforting one another: "Blessed *be* the God and Father of our Lord Jesus Christ, the Father of mercies and God of all comfort, who comforts us in all our tribulation, that we may be able to comfort those who are in any trouble, with the comfort with which we ourselves are comforted by God" (2 Cor. 1:3-4).

If comfort is to be given, engagement must also take place. When someone in your family is hurting, no matter how much you may want to provide comfort, you can't help if that individual refuses to take your calls, come over, or respond to your text messages or emails. They have to allow you in. The same is true for you on your grief journey. You have to allow others in through fellowship and allow them the opportunity to minister to you through the power of the Holy Spirit.

> Not forsaking the assembling of ourselves together, as *is* the manner of some, but exhorting *one another*, and so much the more as you see the Day approaching. (Heb. 10:25)

> Therefore comfort each other and edify one another, just as you also are doing. (1 Thess. 5:11)

I realize focusing on your spiritual health in the midst of this grief journey may at times be the last thing you feel like doing. However, I also know following the G-R-I-E-F formula is certain to usher in increased strength and renewed energy to help you heal. As you grapple to make sense of your new normal, you may be looking for additional practical behaviors to help move you forward. Here are a few to consider:

Be patient with yourself, and give yourself time. Remember there is no timeline for your healing. It takes as long as it takes. Don't put undue pressure on yourself to be better by some predetermined time.

Talk to others who may be experiencing a similar loss. This goes back to the idea of fellowship. Sharing your experience with someone who has had a similar loss can provide tremendous strength, support, and perspective as you heal.

Seek support from friends and loved ones. Your family and friends may not have experienced the loss in the same way you have, but they desire to help you heal. Communicate with them and allow them to support you in ways that are meaningful to you.

Talk to your pastor or other church leaders. Your pastor and other ministry leaders can provide necessary and relevant spiritual guidance during your time of loss.

Seek a qualified professional counselor. Professional counselors possess the skills to walk with you on your journey toward healing. They are able to help you identify areas of greatest concern and assist you in setting goals to move through the grief process.

Accept your feelings for what they are. Feelings are neither right nor wrong; they're merely feelings. They do not define you. Don't beat yourself up for having them, and don't allow others to minimize or overgeneralize yours.

Don't neglect your physical needs (i.e., eat properly, get enough rest). You may not feel like it, but eating properly and getting enough rest can at least help your body feel better. Likewise, not eating properly and neglecting rest can have the opposite effect and cause you significant physical distress. You may not feel up to a full meal, but small portions and healthy snacks may be a great alternative. Even if you can't fall asleep, lay down without the extra stimulation of lights, television, or cell phone. Allow your mind to relax as much as possible.

Avoid using alcohol or other drugs. There may be increased temptation to use alcohol or other drugs to numb your pain. However, recognize these substances may give you temporary relief, but when their effects wear off, you will still be faced with your current situation in addition to a really bad headache!

Avoid making major life decisions for several months. Because your emotions are running pretty high, now isn't the best time to purchase that new car, plot of land, or in my case a new puppy (that's a story for another time). Give yourself time to think clearly. Wait until you are able to make a rational decision minus the emotional high.

Get regular exercise. Exercise is an excellent way to expend some of the negative energy and emotions you are feeling. This does not mean you have to sign up for a half marathon. A regular walk in your neighborhood will do the trick.

Join a support group. You are not alone in your grief, and support groups are a great way to drive this point home. These groups allow you to verbalize your feelings in a safe, supportive environment with others who are processing the same type of loss as you.

Ask for help. No one can read your mind. You know better than anyone else what you are feeling and what you need or want. Ask for what you need, and if you don't know right away, that's OK. Tell your support system, and they may have some suggestions you haven't thought of and are willing to try.

Try to stick to a schedule. Early on in your grief you may have lots of trouble concentrating and staying focused. This can be extremely frustrating and overwhelming. Having a schedule to follow will be beneficial in helping you get needed tasks accomplished.

Write it down. Journaling is an excellent way to make sense of the thoughts ruminating in your head. Getting them on paper will give you an opportunity to begin processing what you're feeling. You may want to start with a particular theme, or just start writing and let your thoughts flow.

Tips for Helping Children and Youth Heal

Encourage their questions and answer honestly. Children will have lots of questions about the loss they experience. Let them know their questions are welcome. Answer honestly about what you know. Don't speculate or give them misleading information and don't be afraid to say, "I don't know."

Listen more than you talk. Young people want to be heard. Ask open-ended questions that require more than a yes or no response. Make sure you listen to what they have to say as well as what they may not be saying. A part of listening is being aware of body language, emotion, tone, and volume.

Let them see your feelings. Children want and need to know they are not alone in their grief. It's OK to express your emotions about the loss you share. This is an excellent opportunity to demonstrate healthy coping skills.

Encourage physical activity. Physical activity is as important to young people as it is for adults. They should engage in age-appropriate play with their peers. Allow them to continue participating in sporting events, extracurricular activities, etc. In short, let kids be kids.

Be flexible about funerals. In the case of loss due to death, attending the funeral is a very personal decision between you and your child. Share with them your thoughts, but give them room to express their concerns and desires. Whatever decision is made regarding their attendance, let them know you support and respect their choice.

Notes

_____
_____
_____
_____
_____
_____
_____
_____
_____
_____
_____
_____
_____
_____
_____
_____
_____
_____
_____
_____
_____
_____
_____
_____
_____
_____
_____

God Help Me, I'm Grieving

_____

_____

_____

_____

_____

_____

_____

_____

_____

_____

_____

_____

_____

_____

_____

_____

_____

_____

_____

_____

_____

_____

_____

_____

Chapter 6

Handling the Holidays

Holidays can be some of the most difficult times to deal with grief. Along with the traditional holiday seasons of Thanksgiving and Christmas, there are others to contend with throughout the year. Mother's Day, Father's Day, birthdays, anniversaries, and other special occasions can all cause feelings associated with grief to spike on or around the holiday. This is not at all uncommon and requires both awareness and a plan of action.

I recall returning to my family home for Thanksgiving after my mother's death. I had not been back to that place since the SUV my husband drove slowly exited my parents' driveway two months prior. We rode in silence as he maneuvered out of the cul-de-sac, holding the steering wheel with one hand and onto me with the other; I stared out the window, hot tears streaming down my face.

The plan was for me and my husband to stay at my parents' home, spend Thanksgiving day at my brother's house, and return to Houston the following day. My knees literally buckled as I turned the key to unlock the front door. My face was wet from the tears that were already flowing as I crossed the threshold and entered the house. As Thanksgiving day came to a close, while relatives trickled out of my brother's home and the return to my parents' home became imminent, I could hold it in no longer. I found myself stretched across the bed in my brother and sister-in-law's room trying to communicate through tears what I could not vocalize with words. I couldn't go back to our parents' house. The pain was too intense. The thought of being there literally made me nauseous. I had pushed myself too far too fast.

Why am I sharing this painful memory with you? Simple. I do not want you to make the same mistake I made during that holiday. I want you to be aware that you don't have to do anything that is too painful. The memories, traditions, and family festivities associated with certain times of year touch us deeply and can naturally cause us to reflect on who or what is no longer part of our lives. You are free to determine how you celebrate or commemorate any particular holiday, if you choose to do so at all.

Dealing with grief during the holiday season or on any special occasion can be a daunting task, but it is one you can overcome. Here are some tips to help you navigate these events without sacrificing your healing:

Plan ahead. Planning ahead can alleviate a large amount of stress associated with the holidays. Remember, there's no right way to grieve, so consider what will nurture your spirit and foster healing during the holiday season. Resist the urge to give in to what others think you should do and stick to what you believe is best for you during the holidays.

Trust God to continue healing your hurt. God has not forgotten you, and he is aware of your pain. Spend time in prayer and meditate on God's word. It will be a source of peace and strength during this and every season.

Acknowledge your pain. It doesn't make you stronger to pretend you're not hurting. In fact, pretending makes the process much more difficult.

Be good to yourself. Get enough rest, and take care of your body by eating and exercising. Don't overindulge in negative behaviors.

Say no. It's OK to avoid the parties, traditions, or festivities you don't feel emotionally ready to engage in. Do the things that you want to do, and say no to the things you don't.

Communicate. Make sure you let those around you know what you need so they know how to best support you.

Don't isolate yourself. As much as you may want to be alone during this time, avoid isolating yourself from others. That doesn't mean you have to attend every party or visit every family member's house. Perhaps you contact one or two close friends or family members for an outing.

Give of your time. This may sound counterintuitive, but giving to others can actually lead to a significant improvement in your mood and overall outlook. Consider volunteering at a local shelter, school, food pantry, hospital, nursing home, or place of worship.

Shake things up a bit. There's no written rule that says you have to celebrate the same way you always have. Change the menu or the location or both. Be open to creating new traditions.

Shop online. If you have become sensitive to crowds during your grief journey, the hustle and bustle of holiday shopping may be too much for you to handle. Avoid the added stress of crowded malls and stores by completing your purchases online.

Have an escape route. Decide before the celebration begins what you will do if your emotions begin to overwhelm you and you need to make a quick exit. Tell at least one other person about your plan. Come up with a signal so they are aware you need some breathing room from the festivities.

Don't overthink it. Sometimes the anticipation can be worse than reality. Don't ruminate over all the things that could go wrong. Try not to determine ahead of time how you'll feel. Take things as they come, and focus on positive healing thoughts.

Enjoy yourself. You may feel guilty about enjoying the holidays because you're "supposed" to be sad. It really is OK to enjoy yourself. If the festivities bring you joy in the midst of moving through your grief, that's a precious gift. Go with it, and don't apologize for having a good time.

Go in for a tune-up. Special occasions are a great time to reconnect with your therapist. A few sessions of brief therapy can be extremely beneficial in helping you gain perspective and tools for coping with your grief.

Tune out negative people. Avoid giving time and energy to people who place unrealistic expectations on you and are not supportive of your grief during this season of difficulty. Surround yourself with family and friends who understand the importance of being present with and for you.

Notes

CHAPTER 7

Moving Forward

Have you ever set out on a road trip that seemed like it would never end? One filled with construction zones, difficult terrain, mistaken exit signs, and wrong turns. There were long, dark roads and a navigation system operating with only minimal connectivity.

Then, the moment you thought you couldn't possibly stand to go another mile, you caught a glimpse of a road sign indicating your desired destination was just beyond the horizon. Relief began to replace exhaustion as you realized your long, arduous, treacherous, painful journey was finally coming to an end.

This is what your grief journey will look and feel like as you move farther away from the pain which has held you hostage for so long. I'm not sure where you are on your road trip with grief. You may be just entering the roadway trying to figure out which direction you should go. Perhaps you've made it through the initial difficult days and weeks and can at least see where you're headed. Or maybe you're nearing the end where an exit ramp is actually in sight.

Wherever you find yourself, I want to encourage you not to give up. Despite the pain you feel now, keep moving. God promises an end to your struggle.

As you get closer to making sense of all you have lost and the toll it has taken on you, you'll begin to see the future much more clearly. What once felt like an oversized blanket smothering you with grief will give way to fresh, new air filling your lungs with life and allowing your eyes to be opened to new possibilities. As you march on toward your new normal, there a few things you can do to ensure a successful arrival at your final destination.

Develop an Eternal Perspective

One of the challenges to healing from loss is the tendency to continue looking in the rearview mirror. There is a struggle with the fear of forgetting about who or what is no longer part of your life. This is usually of greatest hindrance after a loss due to death. The tendency is to resist moving forward or looking ahead due to an erroneous belief that doing so minimizes the level of impact a loved one had on your life. The reality is you won't ever forget your loss, unless you somehow develop amnesia. Although possible, it's highly unlikely.

The Apostle Paul taught about looking toward the future in his letter to the Corinthian church: "For our light affliction, which is but for a moment, is working for us a far more exceeding *and* eternal weight of glory, while we do not look at the things which are seen, but at the things which are not seen. For the things which *are* seen are temporary, but the things which are not seen *are* eternal" (2 Cor. 4:17-18).

Paul's point here was that although you will experience trouble and hardship in this life (to include the pain associated with loss) there is hope for your future. The hope he referred to is the promise of being with Jesus in eternity. The promise of that extraordinary reality far outweighs your current circumstance. It may be difficult to embrace that truth right now, depending on where you are on your grief route. However, your inability to embrace it today will not hinder it from becoming your reality tomorrow.

Moving forward isn't about forgetting at all but remembering with less pain and sorrow. That can't happen if your eyes are focused behind you and locked in on what's been lost. Your goal is to be able to look ahead with renewed vision and eternal perspective.

Take Inventory of What Remains

Part of moving forward after loss will involve you looking around and realizing how much still remains. It's no doubt; in the early stages after loss, it's difficult to see anything other than anguish, despair, or disappointment. That's real, and it's OK. However, along your journey you will need to pause and take an inventory of the people and things still prevalent in your life. This "life inventory" will be a source of encouragement to you as you move closer and closer to healing.

After my mother's death, it was difficult to see through the fog that had become my life over the previous seven months. My world was consumed with interstate travel, doctors' appointments, sleepless nights, hospital stays, and so much more. When it was all said and done, I had to recalibrate my life and figure out how to adjust to my new normal. I wish I could say I did all the right things, but that simply wouldn't be the truth. I messed up quite a bit. Here's why: I was so laser focused on what I no longer had (my mother) that I struggled to give adequate attention to what I did have (my husband and my children).

Let me be clear here; I am not telling you not to take the time you need to grieve. That, after all, is the whole point of this book. What I am telling you is not to lose sight of who and what you still have active and alive in your life as you grieve. In my case it was my family that remained. I now had new opportunities to reconnect with my husband. I had time to give my full attention to my children, particularly my daughter who was in her senior year of high school.

Are there goals you've put on hold? Are there new friendships or relationships you want to pursue? Have you been putting off starting or returning to school? Do you have a dream to start your own business? Is your passport still void of any travel stamps? Is there a ministry burning in your heart?

These are just a few questions to consider as you take inventory of your life after loss. I recognize this may be a tall order depending on where you are along the grief route. It is nonetheless a crucial part of your recovery and long-term healing.

Screen Your Support System

Have you ever been walking down the corridor of a hospital and caught a glimpse of a sign on someone's door with the message "visitors, please check in at the nurses' station"? This typically happens when a patient is receiving a large number of visitors, hampering the ability to heal. The sign is an indication that someone in authority has decided to limit the number of visitors in an effort to allow the patient time needed for a successful recovery.

As well-meaning as family, friends, and loved ones may be, there are times when they can become a distraction to your healing. Here's what I mean. Everybody can't handle your story. Everybody can't handle the depth of your pain. Make certain you are surrounded by a support system capable of handling your grief.

Some people will simply not understand your loss at all and attempt to pull you along too fast. Others will be unable to handle your loss because it reminds them of their own and will attempt to shield you from it altogether. Both will leave you frustrated, unheard, and still in need of healing. Don't be upset with them; it's not their intention to become a distraction. They're simply unable to provide the support you need. Know who they are, and screen them out of the support role for this leg of your journey.

Look for the Lesson

Why? Why did I have to lose my job? Why didn't my relationship work? Why did my marriage end? Why were all of my possessions destroyed in that fire? Why did my loved one die? These are all questions you may be asking as you try to make sense of what has happened. They are healthy and valid because if asked and answered properly they will lead you to the lesson in your loss. It may be impossible to fathom the truth in that statement right now, but there *is* something you can learn from your circumstance—something about you, something about others, or something about God. You may need time to fully discover it, but you can rest assured the lesson is there.

Part of this discovery process begins with embracing the reality that everything has a purpose in God's economy: "And we know that all things work together for good to those who love God, to those who are the called according to *His* purpose" (Rom. 8:28).

This passage of scripture makes it clear that good is on the horizon of your life. You may be struggling to understand how that can possibly be true given the loss you've endured. I wish I could give you the specific, pointed answer you desire, but I would only be grasping at straws. Let me try and explain it the way it was once explained to me.

Have you ever baked a cake? You gather all the ingredients: eggs, butter, flour, vanilla, nutmeg, etc. One by one, you mix them together. After they've been blended and are unable to be distinguished one from the other, you then slide them into a 350°F oven. After a predetermined amount of time, what you remove from the oven is a scrumptious cake to be enjoyed by you and whomever you choose to share it with. Eaten alone, each of the ingredients in that cake would not taste nearly as good as when they are all together. And the cake would not be complete and arrive at its full potential without spending time in the heated oven. *That* is how God works all things in your life for good.

Hopefully, my cake story worked, and you're a bit more open to the truth that even your loss has a lesson. Take the necessary time to identify what it is and then act accordingly. Here are a few tips to help as you move forward knowing your pain has a purpose:

- Ask God to show you the lesson he wants you to learn.
- Use a journal to capture your thoughts on your experience of loss.
- Talk with trusted friends or family members, and ask their opinions.
- Ask yourself the hard questions about your loss.
- Be honest with yourself.

Celebrate Your Arrival

Coming to the end of your grief journey may bring with it some unexpected feelings. You've been on this road for a really long time, and you may be unsure how to feel when it ends. Don't be surprised if you experience a sense of guilt about no longer being consumed with your loss. You may even attempt to hide your newfound feelings of peace for fear of others thinking negatively of you. Give yourself a pass, and let yourself off the hook.

You do not have to linger in your pain. It's OK to celebrate the culmination of a dark and difficult season in your life. Scripture is clear that every occasion you encounter has an allotted time attached to it. Your grief is no exception. Though it seems unlikely, there is an appointed end.

> To everything *there is* a season,
> A time for every purpose under heaven . . .
> A time to weep,
> And a time to laugh;
> A time to mourn,
> And a time to dance.
> (Eccles. 3:1, 4)

Taking into account where you've been and the magnitude of your loss, a time of expressed joy at its finality is warranted. Exaltation at the end of your grief road is an outward expression of an inward realization of God's faithfulness.

When your journey is complete, take some time to look around and soak up the scenery. The sun is shining brighter; the grass is greener; the flowers are in bloom; and the air is lighter. You've endured a long, painful ride that, at times, you weren't so sure you would survive. But the weight of your loss has been lifted, and life is full again.

It's time to smile.
It's time to laugh.
It's time to dance.
It's time to live again.

Notes

Notes

_____
_____
_____
_____
_____
_____
_____
_____
_____
_____
_____
_____
_____
_____
_____
_____
_____
_____
_____
_____
_____
_____
_____
_____
_____
_____

God Help Me, I'm Grieving

_____

_____

_____

_____

_____

_____

_____

_____

_____

_____

_____

_____

_____

_____

_____

_____

_____

_____

_____

_____

_____

_____

_____

Katherine B. Barner

_____
_____
_____
_____
_____
_____
_____
_____
_____
_____
_____
_____
_____
_____
_____
_____
_____
_____
_____
_____
_____
_____
_____
_____
_____

_____

_____

_____

_____

_____

_____

_____

_____

_____

_____

_____

_____

_____

_____

_____

_____

_____

_____

_____

_____

_____

_____

_____

_____

_____

_____
_____
_____
_____
_____
_____
_____
_____
_____
_____
_____
_____
_____
_____
_____
_____
_____
_____
_____
_____
_____
_____
_____
_____
_____
_____

ABOUT THE AUTHOR

Katherine B. Barner is an author, speaker, Bible teacher, and licensed professional counselor. Her focus is on leading and teaching women to grow in Christ. Katherine has a passion for seeing women develop fully into the purpose for which God has designed them. In addition to her love for sharing God's word, she is a staunch advocate of quality mental health treatment with over two decades of experience working in a variety of behavioral health settings. Katherine speaks at workshops, conferences, seminars, and in small group settings. She is a wife, mother, sister, and friend who loves spending time with those closest to her heart. Katherine and her husband reside in Houston, Texas, and are blessed to be parents to four pretty cool young adults.

ORDER INFORMATION

To order additional copies of this book, please visit
www.redemption-press.com.
Also available on Amazon.com and BarnesandNoble.com
Or by calling toll-free 1-844-2REDEEM.

CPSIA information can be obtained
at www.ICGtesting.com
Printed in the USA
BVHW03003510052
579459BV00001B/361